Handy Booklet for Writing

J A BOWLER

First Published by Springtail 2023

Copyright © 2023 J A Bowler

All rights reserved

No part of this book may be reproduced or stored in a retrieval system or transmitted in any form or by any means, electronic, mechanical, photocopying, recording or otherwise without express written permission of the publisher.

J A Bowler asserts the moral right to be identified as the author of this work.

Illustrations by J A Bowler

ISBN: 978-1-8380512-4-2

Handy Booklet for Writing

Dear writer

Welcome to this handy booklet for improving your writing! It is packed with great tips and tricks that you can use every time you sit down to write or edit. This booklet is like having a companion right by your side, helping you find the perfect words and phrases to make your writing stand out and keep your reader interested and engaged. Let's get started!

Dear teacher

As a KS2 UK primary class teacher and English subject leader, I developed a range of resources to support writing. One of these was a useful but rather unwieldy collection of A4 sheets that provided enhanced vocabulary and writing guidance. To make life easier, I eventually consolidated them into a comprehensive booklet that became a must-have for every writing session, helping numerous children improve their texts. The refined version of this booklet is now available as this handy companion for teachers and pupils, containing a carefully curated selection of useful words, phrases, tips, and tricks to take written work to the next level.

Contents

Adjectives

Adjectives describe nouns. They give more detail about the objects, people, places and things in your writing, and help the reader to create a mental picture. Be careful, though. If you use too many, your writing will sound clumsy. You do not need to include them in every sentence.

Adjectives of appearance

adorable	elegant	lovely	scruffy
ancient	fabulous	magnificent	skinny
bare	fancy	mottled	sparkling
beautiful	gorgeous	neat	spiky
brilliant	grizzled	outstanding	stunning
charming	handsome	plain	ugly
cute	incredible	pretty	vibrant
dazzling	jazzy	quaint	wide-eyed
drab	long	radiant	wonderful

*Her **skinny** arms and legs were completely **bare** but on her feet she wore a pair of **spiky** boots.*

Adjectives of character, style or feeling

Positive		Negative	
agreeable	modest	aggressive	intolerant
adventurous	nurturing	aloof	jealous
affectionate	obedient	apathetic	judgemental
amiable	outgoing	arrogant	malevolent
brave	patient	bad-tempered	malicious
careful	playful	bigoted	manipulative
charming	polite	boastful	moody
cheerful	proud	bossy	morose
compassionate	rational	bullying	negative
curious	reliable	callous	obnoxious
delightful	resilient	conceited	patronising
determined	resourceful	confrontational	petty
eager	sensible	contemptuous	petulant
earnest	sensitive	cowardly	pompous
entertaining	shrewd	cruel	predatory
enthusiastic	sincere	deceitful	resentful
faithful	sociable	dishonest	rude
fascinating	sweet	dismissive	shifty
fearless	talented	dogmatic	sneaky
generous	thankful	domineering	sullen
gentle	tidy	egotistical	tetchy
graceful	tolerant	envious	touchy
grateful	tough	fussy	unforgiving
honest	trustworthy	greedy	untrustworthy
humble	understanding	grumpy	vain
imaginative	upbeat	hostile	vindictive
intelligent	valuable	ignorant	violent
inspiring	versatile	impatient	
joyful	vibrant		
knowledgeable	victorious		
lively	warm(hearted)		
lovable	welcoming		
loyal	witty		

Handy tip:
Use adjectives like these to show character by describing a look, an action or speech, e.g. *'He gave her a thankful glance.'*

Adjectives of size

Big		Small	
bulky	mammoth	bite-sized	petite
colossal	massive	compact	pocket-sized
enormous	mighty	dainty	puny
gargantuan	monumental	diminutive	runty
gigantic	mountainous	infinitesimal	stunted
hefty	outsized	Lilliputian	thumb-sized
huge	oversized	microscopic	tiny
hulking	sizeable	mini	undersized
immense	tremendous	miniature	wee
large	vast	minuscule	

Adjectives of sound

annoying	enjoyable	muffled	screeching
calming	explosive	musical	shrill
clanging	faint	muted	silent
chirping	gentle	noiseless	soft
croaky	grunting	peaceful	soothing
deafening	harsh	penetrating	squeaky
deep	hissing	piercing	sweet
dreary	hoarse	rasping	tender
dull	howling	raucous	thunderous
ear-splitting	husky	resounding	tuneful
echoing	low	roaring	unpleasant
eerie	melodic	rumbling	whispered

Did you know many sound adjectives can be made from verbs, e.g. 'a hissing noise'?

The 'calf' (or perhaps it was a 'piglet') was making **gentle, grunting** noises.

Adjectives of texture

abrasive	foamy	oily	slippery
brittle	frozen	padded	smooth
bumpy	furry	papery	soft
bushy	gelatinous	patchy	soggy
chalky	glassy	pebbly	solid
chipped	glossy	peeling	spiky
coarse	grainy	plastic	spongy
cobbled	gravelly	powdery	springy
corroded	greasy	prickly	squishy
cracked	gritty	puffy	stiff
creamy	hairy	quilted	stony
crinkly	hard	ragged	stretchy
crisp	harsh	razor-sharp	stubbly
crumbly	icy	ribbed	supple
crumpled	irregular	ridged	tacky
crusty	itchy	rigid	thick
cushioned	jellylike	rocky	thin
delicate	jumbled	rough	tickly
dense	knobbly	rubbery	tough
dented	knotted	rusty	tufted
doughy	lacy	rutted	uneven
even	leathery	sandy	varnished
feathery	limp	scaly	velvety
firm	liquid	scratchy	watery
flabby	lumpy	serrated	wiry
flaky	metallic	shaggy	withered
flat	molten	sharp	wooden
flexible	mushy	silky	woolly
fluffy	notched	slimy	wrinkled

*Inside was a **slimy, purple** goblin sleeping potion*

Adjectives of colour

red	rust, russet, ruby, crimson, scarlet
orange	pumpkin, umber, ochre
yellow	lemon, canary, gold, mustard, blonde
green	lime, olive, emerald
blue	navy, azure, sapphire, indigo
purple	mauve, violet, lavender
grey	slate, ashy, charcoal, smoky
black	ebony, inky, pitch-black
white	snowy, alabaster, pale, pearly

*An **ancient, rickety** hut stood beside the canal.*

Adjectives of condition

brittle	gritty	permeable	splintered
broken	grimy	polished	steep
burnished	hollow	pristine	strained
corroded	immaculate	relaxed	tarnished
cracked	impeccable	resilient	taut
decrepit	impermeable	rickety	teeming
dim	intact	rigid	tense
empty	jagged	rough	tight
flexible	loose	rusty	tormented
flimsy	lustrous	sagging	uneven
gleaming	malleable	scarred	undulating
glassy	mouldy	shattered	weathered

Adjectives of taste and smell

acidic	foetid	mouldy	smoky
acrid	fiery	musty	sour
antiseptic	fishy	nauseating	spicy
brackish	floral	pungent	stale
bitter	flowery	putrid	stinking
citrus	fresh	rancid	sweaty
creamy	hot	repulsive	sweet
delicious	icy	rotten	tart
doggy	juicy	savoury	tasteless
disgusting	lemony	salty	watery
earthy	minty	sickly	mild

Adjectives of shape

angular	curved	jagged	slender
bent	cylindrical	low	square
broad	deep	lumpy	squat
bulbous	dented	narrow	squiggly
bumpy	flared	oval	steep
chunky	flat	pointy	straight
clunky	high	serrated	twisted
crooked	hollow	shallow	wide
circular	humped	skinny	wavy

Adjectives of time

aged	fast	old	short
ancient	late	old-fashioned	slow
antique	long	quick	swift
brief	modern	rapid	young
early	momentary	recent	youthful

Prepositions

Prepositions tell us the position of something in space or time. These are very useful for story writing, aiding the reader to visualise a scene or action. In non-fiction, prepositions help to make our points clear.

Prepositions			
above	beneath	including	round
across	beside	like	since
after	between	near	through
against	beyond	next	throughout
along	concerning	nowhere	to
amid	considering	of	toward
amidst	despite	off	towards
among	down	on	under
amongst	during	onto	underneath
around	except	opposite	until
as	for	out	up
at	from	outside	upon
before	in	over	with
behind	inside	past	within
below	into	regarding	without

*James sat **on** the bench staring gloomily **at** the murky water, while Dexter paddled **amongst** the scruffy town ducks.*

Adverbs

Adverbs describe verbs or adjectives. They give us more detail about the actions and thoughts of characters. Many of them end in '**ly**' and can be made from adjectives. e.g. **calm+ly=calmly**. Like adjectives, they can enhance your writing and help the reader understand the point you are making or to visualise actions in a story. Try not to overdo them but do remember to include some at the start of sentences to make adverbial openings.

Adverbs

abnormally	famously	miserably	safely
absent-mindedly	fast	mockingly	scarcely
accidentally	fatally	mostly	scarily
acidly	ferociously	mysteriously	sedately
adventurously	fiercely	naturally	selfishly
angrily	fondly	nearly	separately
anxiously	foolishly	neatly	seriously
arrogantly	fortunately	nervously	shakily
awkwardly	frankly	never	sharply
bashfully	frantically	nicely	sheepishly
bitterly	freely	noisily	shyly
bleakly	fully	obediently	silently
blindly	furiously	obnoxiously	sleepily
blissfully	generally	oddly	slowly
boastfully	generously	offensively	smoothly
boldly	gently	officially	softly
bravely	gladly	often	solemnly
briefly	gleefully	openly	solidly
brightly	gracefully	optimistically	sometimes
briskly	gratefully	painfully	soon
broadly	greatly	partially	speedily
busily	greedily	patiently	stealthily
calmly	happily	perfectly	sternly
carefully	fairly	physically	strictly
carelessly	faithfully	loudly	suspiciously
cautiously	hastily	madly	swiftly
cheerfully	healthily	majestically	sympathetically

clearly
cleverly
closely
coaxingly
colourfully
continually
coolly
correctly
courageously
crossly
cruelly
curiously
daintily
delightfully
deeply
defiantly
deliberately
diligently
dimly
doubtfully
dreamily
easily
elegantly
energetically
enormously
enthusiastically
equally
especially
evenly
eventually
excitedly
extremely

heavily
helpfully
helplessly
highly
honestly
hopelessly
hurriedly
hungrily
immediately
innocently
inquisitively
instantly
intensely
interestingly
inwardly
irritably
jealously
joyfully
judgementally
keenly
kindly
knowingly
knowledgeably
lazily
lightly
likely
limply
loftily
longingly
loosely
lovingly
loyally

mechanically
merrily
playfully
politely
positively
powerfully
promptly
properly
punctually
quaintly
questioningly
quizzically
rapidly
rarely
readily
really
reassuringly
recklessly
regularly
reluctantly
repeatedly
reproachfully
restfully
rightfully
rigidly
roughly
rudely
sadly
successfully
suddenly
surprisingly
sweetly

tenderly
tensely
terribly
thankfully
thoroughly
thoughtfully
tightly
too
tremendously
triumphantly
truthfully
ultimately
unfortunately
upwardly
usually
vanishingly
vaguely
verbally
virtually
vividly
warmly
well
wholly
widely
wisely
yearly
yesterday
yet
zealously
zestfully

Triumphantly, *he held up his bill.*

Words to convey feelings

Words that describe physical reactions show what a character is feeling without naming the emotion. The same words can often be used as a verb or a noun.

Words to convey feelings

blush	become red in the face from embarrassment or shyness
clench	tighten a part of the body in anger or anxiety
cringe	shrink or duck in fear or disgust
cry	shed tears of emotion or pain
flare	nostrils become wider in anger
flinch	move suddenly as though about to be hit
flutter	beat quickly and irregularly (e.g. the heart when excited)
frown	bring the eyebrows together in anger, concentration, or anxiety
grin	smile broadly, typically in an informal or unselfconscious way
lurch	sudden movement or feeling (e.g. stomach when scared)
pound	beat forcefully (e.g. the heart when excited or afraid)
recoil	move quickly away from something frightening or unpleasant
scream	high-pitched sound, especially in fear, anger, or pain
shiver	shake as if cold, frightened or wary
shudder	sudden shake from fear or disgust
sigh	exhale audibly in relief, exhaustion or sadness
start	sudden movement from alarm or surprise
sulk	be silent out of annoyance or disappointment
tingle	a tickling sensation in response to fear or excitement
tremble	shake (e.g. knees or hands when afraid)
wince	slight involuntary closing of the eyes as if in pain

*James **recoiled** from the smell as it hit his nostrils.*

Synonyms

Sometimes the first word that comes to mind is the most suitable. The word, 'said', for example, works well when we want a word that does not draw attention to itself. However, if we want to avoid repetition, give variety, or convey meaning more clearly, we can use a synonym. Synonyms are words with similar meanings.

Went

ambled	intruded	proceeded	tapped
bounded	jogged	raced	tiptoed
clambered	journeyed	rambled	toddled
crawled	leaped	rode	tottered
crept	lumbered	rolled	traipsed
cruised	lunged	sailed	tramped
departed	lurched	sallied	trampled
drifted	marched	sauntered	travelled
drove	meandered	scampered	trekked
escaped	merged	scrabbled	trod
exited	moved	scrambled	trotted
flew	navigated	scurried	trudged
galloped	paced	scuttled	tumbled
gambolled	plunged	soared	undulated
glided	pounced	steered	unravelled
hobbled	pounded	strolled	unrolled
hurried	pranced	swept	waded
hastened			

Said

anger	shouted, bellowed, yelled, snapped, thundered, fumed
affection	consoled, comforted, reassured, soothed
excitement	babbled, gushed, exclaimed, cried, whooped
fear	whispered, stuttered, stammered, gasped, urged, hissed
determination	declared, insisted, maintained, commanded
happiness	chirped, giggled, gushed, laughed, cheered
sadness	mumbled, sobbed, sighed, lamented, wept
conflict	argued, disputed, contested, challenged, contradicted
agreement	assented, concurred, nodded, affirmed, acknowledged
amusement	teased, joked, chuckled, chortled, sniggered, giggled
narration	related, recounted, continued, told, recalled, suggested
response	replied, responded, answered, retorted
scolding	rebuked, reprimanded, admonished, chastised

Looked

beheld	squinted	eyed	peeped
glanced	checked out	peeked	saw
cast a glance	laid eyes on	scrutinised	viewed
glared	scanned	surveyed	gazed
peered	stared	gawped	spotted

Common words

angry	irate, annoyed, cross, vexed, irritated, furious, enraged, incensed, fuming, livid, seething
bad	rotten, disappointing, evil, malevolent, malicious, hateful, terrible, awful, wretched
nice	delightful, wonderful, luxurious, charming, gorgeous, delicious
quickly	rapidly, like lightning, without waiting, hurriedly, speedily hastily
sad	unhappy, sorrowful, dejected, miserable, downhearted, despondent, despairing, disconsolate, desolate, gloomy, doleful, dismal
suddenly	at that very moment, all at once, without warning, unexpectedly

The fartlebeast gave a
miserable rumble and **peered**
at them through the gloom.

Further verbs

Well-chosen verbs can really help our readers to understand our meaning and to picture the scenes we are creating. The actual list of verbs is immense – far too long for this handy booklet – but here are forty less common verbs to inspire you.

Forty further verbs with definitions

absorb: take in or soak up (e.g. liquid or information)

bask (in): enjoy a pleasant, warm environment or feeling (e.g. sun, praise)

blend: mix or combine different substances or elements together

clasp: hold tightly with one's hands, arms or a device

cower: crouch down or cringe in fear or shame

crave: have an intense desire or longing for something

dazzle: impress or delight someone greatly by brilliance or excellence

delve: to dig or excavate deeply into something, often figuratively

embark (on): to begin a journey or activity, often with great determination

enchant: delight or captivate someone with charm, magic, or beauty

encourage: give support, confidence, or hope to someone

envelop: wrap or cover something completely

fathom: understand or comprehend something difficult or complex

flicker: shine or move in an unsteady way, often with a quick movement

grasp: seize or hold onto something firmly with one's hand or fingers

guzzle: drink something quickly or greedily, often in large quantities

*Gogzi **clasped** the bars of her cage with both hands.*

halt: stop or pause in movement or progress
huddle: gather closely together, often for warmth or protection
illuminate: light up or brighten, often with knowledge or understanding
inhale: breathe in or draw air or other substances into the lungs
jolt: give a sudden shock or surprise to someone or something
juggle: manage multiple objects or tasks at once, often with great skill
kindle: start or ignite a fire, interest or passion
linger: stay in a place or situation longer than necessary or expected
lunge: make a sudden forward movement, (e.g. with body or a weapon)
marvel (at): be filled with wonder or amazement
nudge: push or prod gently with a slight movement
ooze: flow or seep out slowly, often with a thick or viscous liquid
persevere: persist or continue in a course of action despite difficulties
quench: satisfy a need for something or extinguish a flame
reflect: think deeply about something, often one's own actions
savour: enjoy something fully, often through taste or smell
tackle: deal with a challenge, often with determination or skill
tangle: twist or become twisted together into a confused mass
unleash: set free something, often with great force or effect
unwind: relax or become less tense or anxious
venture (forth): undertake a risky or daring journey or activity
waver: hesitate in making a decision or taking an action
whirl: spin or rotate rapidly, often in a circular motion
yearn (for): have a strong and persistent longing for something

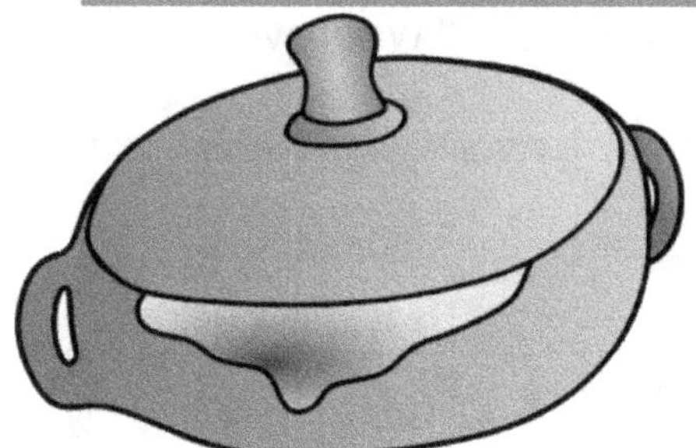

*A sticky, green substance **oozed** out from under the lid.*

Conjunctions

Coordinating conjunctions join words, phrases and sentences to make compound sentences. Subordinating conjunctions make subordinate clauses which, with a main clause, form complex sentences. Using conjunctions means you can create a variety of different sentences types to engage the reader.

Coordinating conjunctions

for	and	nor	but	or	yet	so

Simple sentence 1	Simple sentence 2
James looked through the tunnels.	He could not find Dexter.
Compound sentence	
James looked through the tunnels **but** he could not find Dexter	

Subordinating conjunctions

after	because	provided that	unless
although	before	rather than	until
as	even if	seeing that	when
as far as	even though	since	whenever
as if	if	so that	where
as long as	in order that	supposing	whereas
as soon as	now that	though	wherever
as though	once	till	while

conjunction	subordinate clause	main clause
after	after he found James	Dexter flew out
Complex sentences		
After he found James, Dexter flew out.		
Dexter flew out **after** he found James.		

Sentence starters and linking phrases

You will find these useful in writing non-fiction, or sometimes in fiction when your characters are speaking.

Introduction, support and emphasis

firstly	in the first instance	in which case
to begin with	this is important because	specifically
in other words	it is important to understand	chiefly
notably	the thing to remember is	namely
certainly	another key point is	surely
especially		in fact
in particular		to clarify
with this in mind		for instance

Agreement and addition

additionally	in the first place	as well as
in addition	not only is it… but it is also	together with
similarly	as a matter of fact	of course
furthermore	in the same way	likewise
as	equally important	moreover

Opposition

in contrast	although this may be true	nonetheless
however	of course…, but	regardless
although	on the other hand	notwithstanding
despite	on the contrary	yet
nevertheless	at the same time	even though
conversely	even so	then again

Effect, result and conclusion

consequently	under those circumstances	as shown
as a result	as can be seen	overall
for this reason	in this/that/which case	to sum up
in effect	in the final analysis	in any event
hence	to summarise	in summary
therefore	given that	in conclusion
ultimately	in brief	in short
thus	in the long run	in any case

Purpose, condition and intention

granted that	in the event that	in order to
as long as	for the purpose of	seeing that
in the hope that	on the condition that	seeing as
to the end that	with the intention	in view of
with this in mind	for fear that	if...then
unless	provided that	as
when	given that	due to
whenever	because of this	since

Dear Members of the Council

*I am writing to you **in the hope that** you might do something about the canal which has become badly polluted. **It is important to understand that** this is a key environment for wildlife, but **unfortunately** it is now full of old shopping trolleys and other debris. **Consequently**, it is dangerous and could cause an accident. **Despite** the signs that have been put up, I'm afraid it is worse than ever and **given that** this is a valued local feature, I am sure you will agree that it is worth looking after. **In conclusion**, I hope action is taken so that I am able to return to the water without risking my health or my life.*

Yours

Dexter Duckworth

Checklists for great writing

When you write, you have the freedom to make personal choices. However, knowing what is effective and what to avoid can improve your writing of all text types.

Narrative (stories)

Much of your narrative writing will be 'short stories'. They share many features with longer fiction, but unlike the novels you read, which take months or years to write, short stories need to get to the point and not have too much going on.

Top tips	
Write a powerful first sentence with action, description or dialogue.	✓
Write an opening that nobody else would have thought of.	✓
Start a short story not long before the main event happens.	✓
Write about things you understand and use your own experiences.	✓
Use description to show the reader what to imagine.	✓
Use dialogue (speech) to help the reader know the characters.	✓
Have a point to make or a message to tell.	✓
Have a simple plot with one main focus in one place.	✓
Use a range of sentence types.	✓

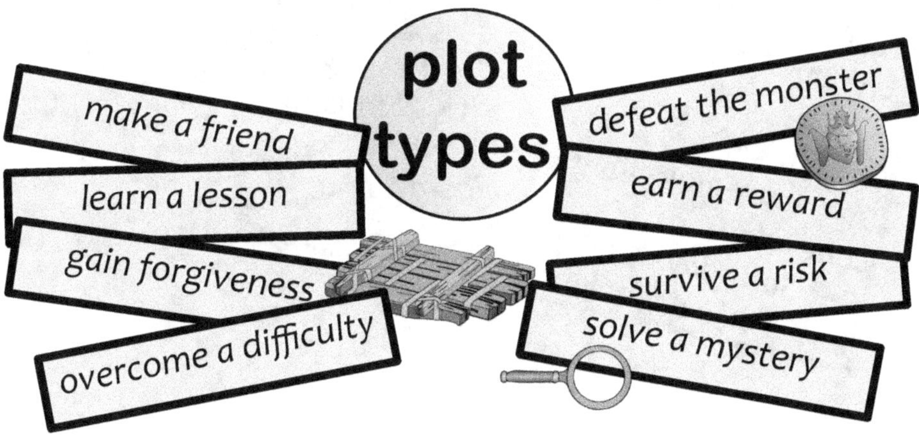

Things to avoid

'Once upon a time' unless it's a fairy story or folk tale	X
ideas and language that have been used many times before	X
lots of pointless background detail	X
themes outside your own experience, e.g. adult romance	X
stories retelling video game play	X
extreme violence, blood and gore	X
pointless conversations between characters	X
too much dialogue – aim for no more than 20%	X
a series of events one after the other without description	X
too many different events and changes of place	X
stating facts instead of showing through action or description	X

Non-fiction

There are many types of non-fiction texts with different purposes. The following 'do' and 'don't' lists will help you achieve the right style and language, but you can also 'bend the rules' sometimes. For example, you may choose to make your language more personal and informal if you are writing for younger children. The key is to have a clear idea of your target reader.

Inform

- Factual text about a topic, e.g. 'Food in Ancient Rome'
- Report of an event
- Newspaper article
- Explanation about how or why something works

Do	Don't
Do write an introduction that says something about the whole topic	Don't write an introduction that is just about the first point
Do organise points into sections or paragraphs	Don't jump back and forth between points
Do use clear, impersonal and mostly formal language	Don't use chatty language or include your own opinions
Do use the sentence starters and linking phrases	Don't use 'over the top' language (hyperbole)
Do use some words that are specific to the topic	Don't use technical terms you don't understand
Do sometimes use quotes and references from other sources	Don't copy from other sources without giving credit (plagiarism)
Do sometimes use subtitles and bullet points	Don't write everything in one long paragraph.
Do use some adverbs and adjectives	Don't use too many adverbs and adjectives
Do think which images would enhance the text	Don't focus on pictures

Persuade

- Advertisement
- Letter asking for something (request)
- Letter of complaint
- Job application
- Election speech
- Call to action for a cause, e.g. 'Save the trees'.

Do	Don't
Do know who you want to persuade	Don't be disrespectful
Do use evidence	Don't claim things that are not true
Do use hyperbole (over the top language) in **adverts, election speeches** and **calls to action**	Don't use hyperbole in **letters of request** or **job applications**
Do use simple and snappy language (including slogans) **for adverts, election speeches** and **calls to action,**	Don't use slogans in **letters** or **job applications**
Do write from your personal point of view in a **letter of complaint or an election speech**	Don't write about your (real) self or your friends or family in **adverts**
Do use the sentence starters and linking phrases	Don't start every sentence in the same way
Do use strong adverbs and adjectives	Don't use very common adverbs and adjectives
Do use imperative (bossy) verbs	Don't use words your reader will not understand

Instruct

- Recipe
- 'How to' article
- Product guide
- Technical manual

Do	Don't
Do write a clear introduction explaining what the instructions are about or giving some background to the subject	Don't jump straight into the first step
Do list equipment needed	Don't write 'you will need' for every item
Do break the instructions down into clear steps	Don't make the instructions long and complicated
Do use numbers or bullet points	Don't write all the instructions in one long paragraph
Do use the imperative form (bossy verbs)	Don't start each instruction with 'you must'
Do present the steps in chronological order (order of time)	Don't jump back and forth between steps
Do give exact details including things like quantities, measurements and timings	Don't assume the reader knows anything about the subject
Do use **prepositions** and **subordinating conjunctions**	Don't make overlong sentences by writing 'and' many times

I would love to see your writing

How did you get on with your latest writing task?

Did you write a story, an article, a letter or something else?

Do you think you managed to make it interesting and engaging for the reader?

Did you edit and improve it, making some careful word choices?

Would you like me to showcase it on my author website?

If so, get an adult to send an electronic version or a photograph of your work to julietbowler@outlook.com with just your first name and your age (no other details, for safety) and I will post it up for others to read!

About the Author

The author is also a writer of fiction for children and young adults. All the characters supporting the examples are from her book:

'The Improbable Adventures of Dexter Duckworth, Part 1: Goblin Earth'.

She is also the author of the **'Ice Cooper'** series of Young Adult supernatural adventures.

The books can be purchased from online retailers and on request from your local bookshop.

More details are available from the author's website:
www.jabowler.co.uk

www.ingramcontent.com/pod-product-compliance
Lightning Source LLC
Chambersburg PA
CBHW071301130726
47998CB00003B/1282